Praise for *Saluting Our Sisters*

From the Judges

"The experience of reading through these engaging, informative and impactful poems was incredibly rewarding. The quality of writing and the range of topics covered were inspiring. I am grateful to all participants for sharing their heartfelt words."

Rob Neil OBE
Director, Krystal Alliance

"It was a great honour to be involved in judging the national BHM poetry competition. There were so many superb entries which demonstrated a breadth and depth of talent across both age categories, from entrants as young as 15 right through to older adults. I really enjoyed seeing how the poems presented different takes on the theme. The quality of the entries made selecting winners and runners-up difficult, but the poems I chose just had that extra special touch. Thanks to all who took the time to enter the competition and share their stories."

Charlotte Shyllon
Founder and Creative Director of Black in White

From the Participants and their Families

"Thank you for the most incredible experience. I can't really put into words how amazing the event was; the atmosphere, solidarity, vibe and poetry was phenomenal, and with that said, I'm so grateful for the opportunity. I felt like somebody and I had a purpose. I loved it. Thanks to you and your colleagues, I have had one of the best times of my life and made an everlasting memory for myself and my family. You should be very proud of yourself. With Love and Kindness."

RS

"I would like to thank you for the amazing reception at the House of Commons and the great honour Ione received winning her category, particularly that it was chosen by Joseph Coelho. Her school submitted the poem and I wasn't very prepared for the whole event, but it was absolutely fantastic. Congratulations on organising such a wonderful competition and all the hard work that had clearly gone into it."

Mother of one of the winners

Saluting Our
Sisters

Compiled by
Cherron Inko-Tariah MBE

(and Friends)

First published in Great Britain in 2024
by Book Brilliance Publishing
265A Fir Tree Road, Epsom, Surrey, KT17 3LF
www.bookbrilliancepublishing.com

© Copyright Cherron Inko-Tariah MBE 2024

The moral right of Cherron Inko-Tariah MBE to be identified as the author of this work has been asserted in accordance with the Copyright, Designs and Patents Acts 1988.

All rights reserved. No part of this publication may be reproduced, stored in a retrieval system, or transmitted, in any form or by any means without the prior written permission of the publisher, nor be otherwise circulated in any form of binding or cover than that in which it is published and without similar condition being imposed on the subsequent purchaser.

A CIP catalogue record for this book is
available at the British Library.

ISBN 978-1-913770-91-4.

Editing by Olivia Eisinger
Design, typesetting and proofreading by Zara Thatcher

To all black women…

Whoever you are, wherever you are,
this anthology is dedicated to you.

Contents

Foreword	1
Introduction	3
The Seacole Group	7
The Winning Entries	11
The Finalists	25
Highly Commended	61
Contact BHM magazine	149

Foreword

Joseph Coelho OBE FRSL

Saluting Our Sisters is a poetry anthology to be savoured. It is an invitation to think about, pay tribute to, honour and learn about the lives of Black women over the centuries. So many accomplishments of Black women have gone horrifically unsung. This collection, brought together by Cherron Inko-Tariah MBE, addresses this injustice by highlighting hugely inspiring Black women.

You will find poems about well-known names such as Mary Seacole who, as one of the winning entrants, Ione Knight puts it, *""...there she stood, A spot of black in a sea of white"*. Other famous names include civil rights activist Maya Angelou and the incredible Harriet Tubman and her Underground Railroad. However, there are also poems about Black women you may not be familiar with, such as journalist and activist Claudia Jones who was vital in founding the Notting Hill Carnival, mathematician Katherine Johnson and her 33-year-career at NASA, and Sislin Fay Allen, the first Black women police constable in the UK.

These are stories I wish I knew growing up, stories that would have placed my family and, by extension, me, in the history books. Time and time again, we hear how important it is to see ourselves and each other reflected in film, TV and books. Whilst moves have been made in this direction, we still, sadly, have a long way to go. Collections such as *Saluting Our Sisters* are vital to help everyone learn about and benefit from the knowledge of our shared histories and contributions to society. As one of the contributors, Zoe Sheaf, beautifully puts it, we can all…

"… salute the silence.
The absences and the shadows,
The ripped-out thread from history's tapestry."

Joseph Coelho OBE FRSL

Joseph is a British poet and children's author who was Children's Laureate 2022-2024. He is a Fellow of the Royal Society of Literature and won the Carnegie Medal for his YA novel *The Boy Lost In The Maze* in 2024.

Introduction

Having written for the BHM magazine over the last few years, I wanted to get more involved. So when an opportunity rose for me to take on the role as Editor-in-Chief at the start of 2023, I jumped at it!

One thing I knew I wanted to do was to celebrate Black women. When I announced that the theme for BHM 2023 was 'Saluting our Sisters', I cannot tell you the number of questions and queries this raised; Why Black women?

I could say that highlighting the achievements and contributions of Black women throughout history does not mean we are ignoring Black men.

I could say that for centuries, the voices of Black women have been suppressed, silenced and sidelined.

I could say that the application of adultification bias results in the rights of Black girls being diminished or ignored, #ChildQ.

I could say that a Black woman is five times more likely to die during childbirth (in the UK).

I could say that Black women are deemed unprofessional when we wear our hair in its natural condition or protective styles (but these hairstyles are accepted when donned by women of other ethnicities!).

I could talk about Black femicide and how this is not given the attention it deserves and the insidious minimisation of violence against Black women that can't be ignored.

I might even say that it's because our bodies have been ridiculed (Sarah Baartman), used for medical experiments or cells removed from our bodies without permission (Henrietta Lacks).

I could say all of this and more because it is all true. But my response to the question 'Why Black women?' is a simple one…

Why not Black women?

This anthology is a selection of poems written by people of different ages, ethnicities and backgrounds, but they all share one thing in common: they have used their creative gift to elevate and celebrate the beauty, talent, intelligence, power and wonder of Black women.

About BHM

Black History Month magazine is a national annual magazine. www.blackhistorymonth.org.uk is the central point of focus and leads the nationwide celebration of Black history, arts and culture throughout the UK every October.

Why 'Saluting Our Sisters'?

Black women have shaped history and inspired change, making profound impacts in various spheres including literature, religion, music, fashion, sport, business, politics, academia and healthcare.

The BHM platform wanted to shine a light on the outstanding Black women who have been pivotal in transformative social justice movements throughout history, but their courageous contributions have often been overshadowed or neglected. 'Saluting Our Sisters' was about correcting this.

The Competition

BHM magazine hosted a national BHM poetry competition as a tribute to the invaluable contributions of Black women, bringing to the forefront the emerging poetic talents from young people and the African and Caribbean communities.

Engaging over 3,000 poets across the nation, the competition highlighted the indispensable role of poetry in fostering education and cultural expression.

Our panel of judges included Joseph Coelho OBE (Children's Laureate 2022-2024); Charlotte Shyllon, founder and creative director of Black in White; and Rob Neil OBE, founder and director of Krystal Alliance.

From an overwhelming number of submissions, a panel of esteemed judges shortlisted 105 exceptional poems, with 17 talented poets advancing to the final stage and 4 winners selected.

Being involved in this poetry competition was an absolute delight. The diversity and passion in the submissions were outstanding. A heartfelt thank you to everyone who contributed to making this competition a success.

The winners were announced at a special Winners' Reception at the House of Commons hosted by Marsha de Cordova MP on World Poetry Day, 21st March 2024, and during International Women's month.

Cherron Inko-Tariah MBE
Editor-in-Chief, BHM Magazine

I am delighted that the Seacole Group is able to support the National Black History Month Poetry Competition, by contributing to the publication of an anthology of so many impactful poems about Black women and their sometimes forgotten or ignored pivotal role in our society.

It is vital that the stories of these female icons are amplified and shared so that we may learn the power of inclusion by recognising the Black women in our history and in our nation's narrative.

It is also apt that Ione Knight's poem, the winner in the children's category, has captured so powerfully the spirit and legacy of Mary Seacole, our namesake.

It is such an honour to be able to support young and emerging talent in the field of poetry, one of the most creative and compelling forms of the written word.

I salute all of those that were involved in creating such an inspiring and successful competition, and to all of those involved in coming up with and crafting such wonderful work.

Sim Scavazza

Chair, The Seacole Group

The national network for Black, Asian and ethnic minority Chairs and Non Executive Directors in the NHS

https://www.seacolegroup.com

THE WINNING ENTRIES

CHILDREN

Mary Seacole: Braver Than a Soldier
A Nurse Ready To Save Lives
by Ione Knight

YOUNG TEENS

Resilient Queens: A Salute to Our Sisters
by Ebunoluwa Allen

OLDER TEENS

Sadie Alexander
by Sasha Cummings

ADULTS

Yes We Can
by Marie Williams

CHILDREN

Mary Seacole: Braver Than a Soldier
A Nurse Ready to Save Lives
by Ione Knight

On the edge of London,
there she stood,
A spot of black in a sea of white.
On the edge of London,
there he stood,
Blending in a sea of cowards
Both ready to risk everything.
"You can't do it, just come back," her friends pleaded.
She shook her head, "Courage is the one thing I do not lack."
"You won't make it, you won't come back,"
his friends murmured.
He shook his head, "I need to pack."
He pulled on his helmet – too scared to show his face.
She pulled on her cap – too kind to hide her face.
He hefted a gun.
She held a bandage.
Both ready to risk everything.
He wore a shining medal that read: Bravery.
She wore a red cross and a name that read: Mary.

YOUNG TEENS

Resilient Queens: A Salute to Our Sisters
by Ebunoluwa Allen

In October's embrace, we stand tall and proud,
Saluting our sisters, their voices so loud.
Through history's pages, their strength shines bright,
Guiding us forward like stars in the night.
From Sojourner Truth's resolute call,
To Maya Angelou's poetic thrall,
Our sisters have shaped a story untold,
A legacy of courage, strong and bold.
Harriet Tubman, a conductor of hope,
Leading the way, helping others to cope.
Rosa Parks, on that bus, took her stand,
With a simple act, she changed our land.
Shirley Chisholm, the first in the chair,
Breaking barriers with passion to spare.
And let's not forget Fannie Lou Hamer's fight,
For civil rights with all of her might.
This month, we celebrate these queens of the past,
Their perseverance and spirit unsurpassed.
In Black History Month, we sing, and we say,
Salute to our sisters in a mighty display.

OLDER TEENS

Sadie Alexander
by Sasha Cummings

Lost in the white pages of "Econ 101",
in lecture theatres and honorary libraries,
is Sadie Alexander, the Economist.

Pigeon-holed as another civil rights activist,
she is nowhere to be found in Economics.

Yet, absent in the minds of countless generations,
is the recognition of the *tragic irony*
of the woman who fought tirelessly
for the fair standards of the living;
being treated so unfairly in both life and death.

Missing is the outrage of the first African-American woman
in history to achieve a PhD in Economics, being punished
        out
           of the profession
for not being born a "Karl", "John", or "Adam".

All the collective disgust and frustration we should
feel for her indefensible mistreatment,
    goes unfelt.

This injustice, in itself, is an outrage.

How many more Sadies need to suffer?

Smothered into silence
by the cruel, decisive hands of history;
of textbook writers that seem to have an appetite
for an army of wealthy, white-wig-wearers,
dictating the theory taught to Sadies across the globe.

How much more brilliance will go untouched,
collecting dust alongside painfully pointless PhD
diplomas?

That is why her name and her economic contributions must be said.
Written.
Read.
Heard.
Spoken.
Learned.

Her name must be the title of not only this poem but many more.

May it branch out into plaques under park monuments.

May it be written in **black, bold** contrast to the pale pages that have composed Economics thus far.

May names like Sadie's be interwoven into teachings all year round,
>   not solely plucked out
>   in October, fleeting
then quickly disposed of
alongside Halloween decorations.

May the next generation of possible Sadies
Free themselves
not from her ambition, but from her fate.

ADULTS

Yes We Can
by Marie Williams

Black women, You span the world
You span the universe, You span the continents.

You span the villages, You span your homeland,
And across these spans, All your achievements
Worthy to be praised.

As black women, challenges
Have often befriended you
Wrapped in othering by society
Taught to be illiterate, expected to tantalise
The groins and hearts of men
Your black beauty unseen.

And when all this became unbearable
You broke the shackles of bondage,
You broke the years of heartache and disdain.
You began to rise
Gifted and blessed.

You walked through a series of doors
Conquering political, racial and social justice,

No longer a mere home-maker,
But a trailblazer in business, innovation, and entrepreneurship
You, a raconteur, An author, A poetry performer.
You, a publisher, Defying the status quo

Made you creative and confident.
Imagine the misogynists
Sitting on their verandas
Questioning who authorised you,
To become experts in Stem –
Science, technology, engineering, mathematics

How absurd!
For you all, there is no looking back
As you turn up the volume
Dancing to a yes we can tune.
Redressing the imbalance
Empowering future generations
To aspire, achieve and soar
As they prepare to walk in your footsteps.

THE FINALISTS

CHILDREN

First

It is Hard
by Ananya Pawar

Second

A Girl's Dream
by Mia Johal

Third

Harmony of Voices:
Celebrating Black Women in Poetry
by Ivaan Agnihotri

YOUNG TEENS

Joint First Finalist

Reflecting Black Women:
Celebrating Strength, Resilience, and Success
by Ama Owusu

Joint First Finalist

A Light in the Dark
by Nell Ost

Second Finalist

Black Women Shine
by Eshan Adeel

Third Finalist

I'm Truly in Awe
by Keichardae Walters

OLDER TEENS

First Finalist

I Salute
by Zoe Sheaf

Second Finalist

Wonder Women
by Yohana Gasu

Third Finalist

Toni Morrison
by Jamie Shaw

ADULTS

First Finalist
Potter's Clay
by Teena Mabry

Second Finalist
ME
by Jennifer Townsend

Third Finalist
Dear Black Woman
by Rae Snowden

CHILDREN

First Finalist

It is Hard
by Ananya Pawar

To be where you are is Hard,
To try to be treated fairly as a Woman is Hard,
To try to be treated as a Black person is Harder,
To be Yourself is Harder,
To stand up and say that you matter is Harder,
But trying to be it all
is the Hardest Thing Ever.

Second Finalist

A Girl's Dream
by Mia Johal

The room is dark,
The room is cold,
I try to sleep.
I want to dream of life beyond my dangerous street…

I want to sparkle, shine and sing like Beyoncé.
Her glamour and smile fill the room with hope.

Or could I be Simone or Serena, both from different worlds,
But both are so strong, determined and never give up.

Putting fame and fortune aside, maybe my future is Rosa Parks
Fearless, stubborn and filled with self-belief.
A story from ordinary to extraordinary!

Dawn breaks, and the next day brings light, hope and new beginnings.
It is up to me to create my History.

Third Finalist

Harmony of Voices:
Celebrating Black Women in Poetry
by Ivaan Agnihotri

In the heart of February, a time to remember
National Black History Month, like glowing embers,
A tribute to the past, a path we retrace,
To honour the lives that have left their trace.

But this year's celebration, a radiant theme,
Celebrating black women like a radiant dream.
In a poetry competition, voices will soar
To honour their stories, we open the door.

For the power of words, a lyrical dance,
Shall pay homage to women, their strength and their stance.
In a world that's oft harsh, their voices shine bright,
Their resilience and grace are an inspiring sight.

From Harriet Tubman, who led to her own,
To Maya Angelou's words, like seeds that are sown,
These women, like stars, in history's grand sky
Guide us through darkness, inspire us to fly.
The ink of their legacy, on pages now spread,

Through verses and stories, their spirits are led,
To remind us of courage, of talent, of grace,
In a world where they thrived in every place.

Their contributions, vast and profound,
In arts, science, and change, they astound,
With wisdom and brilliance, they paved the way
For future generations to thrive and to say:

*"We celebrate black women, so strong and so true,
Their stories inspire, their voices imbue,
With hope and knowledge, we honour their name,
In this poetry competition, we play the same game."*

So let us embrace, with pen and with heart,
This gathering of talent, where stories impart,
The beauty, the strength, the grace and the might,
Of black women who shone through history's night.

In celebration and learning, together we stand,
As the words of their legacy echo through the land.
For in poetry's embrace, we unite and commend,
The spirit of black women, our sisters and friends.

YOUNG TEENS

Joint First Finalist

Reflecting Black Women: Celebrating Strength, Resilience, and Success

by Ama Owusu

Black women, they are queens so rare,
With strength and beauty beyond compare.
Their dark-skin, a testament of history
Resilient and bold, a symbol of victory.

In the face of adversity, they rise above,
Their voices echo with power and love.
From the struggles of the past, they've emerged strong,
Defying expectations, proving them wrong.

They carry the weight of generations past,
Their stories untold, their voices vast.
Mothers, daughters, sisters, and friends,
Their bond unbreakable; the love never ends.

They are the true embodiment of grace,
Navigating life's challenges with style and pace.

Their talents and achievements, a sight to behold,
In every field, their brilliance is untold.

So let us celebrate the black women today
For their strength and resilience on full display
They are the pillars of our communities true,
With boundless potential, there's nothing they can't do.

Joint First Finalist

A Light in the Dark
by Nell Ost

A light in the dark,
A voice in the silence,
She made her mark,
She fought without violence.

A candle burning bright,
A word spoken with truth,
She was a spark ready to ignite,
Her flame started in youth.

A warrior in battle,
A poet holding a pen,
She wrote with such attal,
She's needed now and back then.

Audre Lorde, a student,
Audre Lorde, a teacher
Audre Lorde was prudent,
Audre Lorde was the preacher.

Audre Lorde, have you heard?
Audre Lorde, do you know?
Do you know she was a light?
Do you know she was a voice?

A mark?
A fight?
Do you know she was a warrior?
A student and teacher?
A poet or a preacher?

She needs to be known.
She needs to be heard.
So I write this poem,
So her words can be learned.

A light in the dark,
A voice in the silence,
She made her mark
She fought without violence.

Second Finalist

Black Women Shine
by Eshan Adeel

In a world that tries to dim their light,
Black women shine with all their might.
With grace and power, they stand tall,
Breaking down barriers, they conquer all.

Their voices echo, loud and clear,
Inspiring hearts, dispelling fear.
From their roots, a legacy grows,
A testament to the strength they bestow.

In every stride, they redefine,
Beauty, intelligence, so divine.
With resilience as their guiding force,
Black women rise, their power endorsed.

So let us celebrate their grace,
In every shade, in every space.
For black women, we proudly cheer
In their presence, greatness is near.

Third Finalist

I'm Truly in Awe
by Keichardae Walters

Black women in history I adore,
Harriet Tubman, Maya Angelou and even more,
Boldness, resilience you see, I can't even keep score,
A true inspiration, Claudia Jones
A journalist, activist, feminist and who knows
Sojourner now here's the Truth: a courageous woman
we all should know
her strength and determination is truly contagious
so let's stand tall and salute.
Escaped slavery with no help at all
truly uplifting: that's what she is
Black women in history I adore
Tubman, Angelou, Jones, Truth and many, many more.
Their skin, hair, eyes all vary in colour
but one thing I know for sure
these women are so intellectual
I'm truly in awe.

OLDER TEENS

First Finalist

I Salute
by Zoe Sheaf

I salute the silence.
The absences and the shadows,
The ripped-out threads from history's tapestry.
The hole in my heart that tells me something…
Someone
Is missing.

I salute
Those who fought before,
Those who fight now
And those who will fight on
Unknown and unrecognised.

I salute all
Who do not
Strive for a glorious chapter of history's pages,
But simply do it
Because it is right.

I salute the ghosts
Of women whose writing is lost,
Of women who fought in long-forgotten battles,
Of women who strode into now extinguished lights
Of women
Black women.
I salute them every day.
The woman who cuts my hair;
The woman who passes me in the street;
The woman who serves me at the till.
I see the secret stories hidden in their eyes.
No one will know them.
But there is power in their anonymity.

I salute all the
Artists, businesswomen, models, poets, authors, politicians, activists
Lost in the gaps between the floorboards of history,
Scrubbed out by the dictators of our past
Who found them,
Too brave, too loud, too fierce, too bold!

I salute my sisters
From every walk of life, from every country,
Those who I know
And those who I will never meet.

I salute with hope
That one day
The silence
Will end.

Second Finalist

Wonder Women
by Yohana Gasu

Women, do you wonder about your history?
About the stories and the lullabies of legacies;
The tales of those who pioneered the present you've received.
Who overcame adversity to present you with this opportunity.
You rode the great railroad she paved below the plains.
You are the product of a generation once enslaved.
Your injuries and wounds all treated by her expertise.
Despite the prejudice she faced, she attended to your every need.
She saw that "the freedom gates [were] still [but] half ajar."
Her endeavours have led to women now being where they are.
Through her masterful manipulation of organic chemistry
She brought to you a brand-new treatment for leprosy.
Her cosmetics and hair products cultivated unseen opulence,
And this entrepreneurial philanthropist gave out of her abundance.

She was the first to obtain her long-sought college degree,
As a result, her name remains engraved in history.
Her mathematical prowess was beyond comprehension.
This human-computer was vital in spearheading space exploration.
Her supreme performance in Motown was a sight to behold,
Now, no mountain is high enough to stop you from reaching your goals.
From the Paris university, she received her PhD.
One cannot, therefore, dismiss her academic prestige.
Through the Bible, the bath and the broom, she educated many women,
Showing you that your role extends far beyond the kitchen.
For thirty years, they denied her accredited patent,
But her sanitary belt was a revolutionary development.
She was the Democratic nominee for the US Presidency;
Taking a resolute stand for economic, social and political equality,
Her poetry and autobiographies were pieces of literary mastery
Rising above all acts of abysmal adversity.

I wonder about these women and all others
incarcerated by ignorance
Whether what they have done for you has any
substantial significance.
Yet each one has paved a new path for us to perceive so
Women wander further down the road of history.

Third Finalist

Toni Morrison
by Jamie Shaw

Red hot molten metal
That could scar the skin for life.
Lumps of iron that refuse to mould
Under even the most powerful blows.
From the trauma that hangs over 124 Bluestone Road
To Pecola's adoration for Shirley Temple,
Toni's armour is frightening, admirable and beautiful;
As the armourer bends raw iron into shiny cuirasses
They both dazzle in their beauty
And defend the soldier from attack,
Toni Morrison forms crude words into language.
Never let it be tarnished by the wind and rain.

ADULTS

First Finalist

Potter's Clay
by Teena Mabry

Black Woman.
I see you.
I see your skin with its beautiful shades of brown, black, and hints of red,
cinnamon, peanut butter, dark chocolate, or yellow as cornbread.
Like Black Men, you were taught that showing raw emotion is frowned upon,
They don't want to know or see you but to see enough to get turned on.
But take a moment to look past that flawless skin, perfected through fire and
You will see her value runs deep.
She is that whole package, meant for you to keep…
safe.

Black woman.
I see you.
You have worked backbreakingly hard, born with two backbones.

When one is splintered by ignorance, hate, disappointment, and the desire to fit in
You have another one to pull yourself up, stand on your own, and lean in.
God knew you were something special, the mothers of the earth.
Remember who you are, and do not forget that you were birthed from potter's clay.
Your name is Queen.

Second Finalist

ME

by Jennifer Townsend

I am a beacon of light in the darkness
I sometimes carry the burdens of the world on my shoulders
But I never give up or give in
I remember where I come from and where I am going
Sometimes, when others look at me
They see my womanhood and my 'Blackness.'
They don't see ME
Why is that? I wonder,
Is my mask so good that I am invisible?
I know I am not invisible because when I look in the mirror
I see ME
I see colour
I see many shades
'Black' is what they want me to be
They want to stereotype and categorise me.

However, I cannot be stereotyped or categorised
Why? Because I am ME
Strong and weak
Resilient and fragile

Loud and quiet
Happy and sad…
I am diverse
I wear many disguises
However, when I take them all off
When I strip down to ME
What I am left with is
Beauty
Beauty that transcends all
Beauty that is love
Beauty that is light
I am a Woman
I am ME

Third Finalist

Dear Black Woman
by Rae Snowden

In years to come, will we still think of black women as different
In years to come, we will still think of black women as irrelevant
If the past is a lesson worth learning, we must learn from the wrongs
If the past is a lesson worth learning, we must learn from their songs
The songs that sing a lifeline deep into our souls
The songs that sing a melody lifting our lows
Their words gave us encouragement, hope, rhythm and groove
Their words gave us a feeling, making our bodies move
Their music is our medicine for the days we need some peace
Their music is our medicine for when we need some beats
I wonder if the black woman knows her songs speak so much
I wonder if the black woman knows her songs have a heavenly touch

Dear black woman, you sing a song so powerful.
Dear black woman, you sing a song so colourful
Do you know you reach so many with your sweet serenity?
Do you know you reach so many with your chosen destiny?
God has blessed you with a soulful voice
God has blessed you and with that, we rejoice
Always singing loud despite the negatives
Always singing loud despite their narratives
Using your voice to heal the crowd
Using your voice to make us proud
You are every woman; you are a survivor
You are a natural woman; you are the girl on fire
Standing together United, we salute you, sister, with love
Standing together, United sister, we thank the lord above.

HIGHLY COMMENDED

CHILDREN

Inspirational
by Kara Kambli

1 2 3 Count on Katherine
by Maya-Sophia Nielsen

Rachel Renée Russell
by Pola Guzniczak

Beautiful Women
by Raastin Riazi Pachenari

Recipe 1: How to Make a Phenomenal Woman
by Willow Beal

Celebrating Black Women – Hidden Figures
by Adeife Fajobi

Steps to Success
by Sofia Karayannis

Black Women History
by Ehab Shahnawaz

Sislin Fay Allen
by Eshan Ambrose

YOUNG TEENS

Be Black and Proud
by Lannaya Wilks

Mary Seacole: While the Bombshells Fall
by Isabella Hope-Smith

Celebrate Black History
by Tehrim Fatima

SHE
by Narcisca Zaharia

Mary Seacole
by Jack Holland

The Magazine
by Lili Guthrie

Saluting Sisters: A Tribute to Black Women in History
by Nosheen Akhtar

Women Empowerment
by Summer Casson

Imagine…
by Eliza Krause

She Is
by Grace-Petra Quainoo-Abban

Sitting Down to Stand Up – Rosa Parks
by Darci Lee-Smith

We are Black Women
by Isabelle Ahanon

From a Black Girl to a Black Woman
by Yvette Wamala

OLDER TEENS

Shine
by Elizabeth Okunola

Grace
by Ronav Bhanot

This Black Soul
by Natasha Gachuma

Saluting our Sisters
by Lorna Kerr

Michelle Obama
by Dora Glass

Whispers of Anastacia
by Pakeeza Noor

My Identity
by Princess Martins

Her Hidden History
by Felicity Whele-Plummer

Black History Month
by Pranav Yadav

Inspirational Black Women
by Sabooh Ahmed

ADULTS

Afraid to be Alone, but Wanting to be Free
by Rebecca McLeod

CHILDREN

Inspirational
by Kara Kambli

R is for Resourceful, like Harriet Tubman, fighting to abolish slavery.
O is for Observant, like Katherine Johnson, the maths professor at NASA.
S is for Saintly, like Saint Josephine, the first black female saint.
A is for Artistic, like Maya Angelou, the poet.

P is for Pioneering, like Mae Carol Jemison, the first black woman to go to space.
A is for Astonishing like Kamala Harris, the US vice-president.
R is for Regal, like Aretha Franklin, the queen of soul music.
K is for Kind-hearted, like Michelle Obama, inspiring others with her writing.
S is for Superb, like Serena Williams the greatest ever tennis player.

You must never be fearful about what you are doing when it is right."
- Rosa Parks

CHILDREN

1 2 3 Count on Katherine
by Maya-Sophia Nielsen

Katherine Johnson a mathematician, best in her prime.
A computer at NASA, all in time.
Questions were her inventions.

Some numbers can make important numbers.
Astronauts guided by the stars.
Katherine's calculations almost made it to Mars.

Space race to calculate Friendship 7 to the moon.
Apollo 13 relies on women to make dreams shine.

Boundless and curious caught the attention of the President.
Medal of Freedom for a ground-breaking black American.

CHILDREN

Rachel Renée Russell
by Pola Guzniczak

Dork Diaries are my favourite books
They attach to me like hooks.
Nikki's adventures fill my mind
I can read them all the time.

Book creator Mrs Russell
Spent her childhood in a bustle.
There were five kids in her crib
Number 1 was on her race bib.

Being an author was her dream
So she made up a little scheme
And signed up for a writing course.
She worked hard like a horse.

A vicious tutor smashed her dream.
Their cruel words cut off her wings,
"If I never reach the top
I'll give up this kind of plot."

So she went to work elsewhere
She was great at this, I swear.

But writing tempted her so much,
It never got out of her clutch.
She put some stories from her life,
And her daughters', into lines;
That's how Dork Diaries began,
A few more books were written soon.

Rachel shows if you believe.
Your superpower is a gift.
Sooner or later, dreams can come true
So stick with your passion hard as glue.

CHILDREN

Beautiful Women
by Raastin Riazi Pachenari

Wonderful women,
Ocean of Love,
Magnificent mothers,
Amazing aunts,
Nurturing nans.

The power of mind
Risen from the dark
Stood up for humankind.
The earth is a mother
The moon is a girl
The sea is a woman.

Resilient Rosa
On the bus,
Heroine Harriet
Leading to Freedom,
Fighting Fannie Lou
Got the vote.

All beautiful, black women
Strong and determined
Here's a poem for all women
Woman, life, freedom.

CHILDREN

Recipe 1: How to Make a Phenomenal Woman
by Willow Beal

Talent is first in the pot,
Let it melt and bubble,
Shake in some of Simone Biles' resilience,
Now add fresh independence,
Let it simmer for two minutes.
Then, add the smartness of Katherine Johnson,
Sieve in power, then let it prove for an hour.
Note: patience is the key, and if you do not let it settle,
It will become sad, cold and deflated.
Splash in creativity from Ava DuVernay
And blend in a star.

Allow time to cool.

Now add your preserved expression and stir vigorously,
Leave for a day, and then remove the mixture from the pot.
Knead in bravery, then put in the oven for eight hours,
Take out of the oven and sprinkle with generation,
Serve with sweet honour and enjoy!

CHILDREN

Celebrating Black Women – Hidden Figures
by Adeife Fajobi

We are ornamented pillars in society
The backbone of the home
The unseen drummers in the Dance of Life
Fertile, productive, progressive, and Brainiac,
Who are we?

We are roses, beautiful and elegant,
Survive the piercing thorns.
Though our drums be silenced
Our dance is visible!
Who are we?

We birthed various things:
Music, media, sports, science and others
Who are we?

We are Black Women
We boost the economy
Most under-celebrated, less-educated
In war, sickness and pain
We stay strong

We may be hidden,
Our tears unseen
Our voice is louder
We can't be ignored but be celebrated.

CHILDREN

Steps to Success
by Sofia Karayannis

Shake
a pot of independence, season with astronomy,
sieve some curiosity and you get…
Katherine Johnson.

Unite
a pinch of power of passion,
peel in creativity
and that's the recipe for
Ava DuVernay.

Combine
a flourish of books and scripts,
preserve a punch of joy and love,
bring to the boil and serve,
Maya Angelo.

Cook
some courage and compassion,
now preserve the wisdom,
pour in a pack of Idol flour,

and you've created
Rosa Parks.

Even
out the fun and joy,
weigh the ideas,
Burn away the sadness, and you've made
Beau H.

Sieve
in the bravery,
knead the strength
and you get
Success for all.

CHILDREN

Black Women History
by Ehab Shahnawaz

In days of old, when tales were told
And legends lived and breathed,
Black women stood tall, their stories untold.
Their feats and deeds unleashed.

Their beauty, like the sun in the sky,
Shone bright, their spirit did not die,
In the face of oppression, they did not cry,
Their strength, a beacon, did not die.
From the fields of cotton to the halls of power,
Black women rose, each hour,
Their voices, a melody, did not cower,
Their hearts aflame, with every flower.

From Harriet to Angela to Maya,
Their names etched in history's bay,
Their courage, a guiding light, did not sway,
Their determination, a beacon, did not stray.

In the face of adversity, they did not bend,
Their resilience, a testament, did not end,

Their legacy, a gift, did not descend,
Their love, a river, did not pretend.

In the face of hate, they did not falter,
Their hope, a flame, did not halt,
Their dreams, a vision, did not scatter,
Their spirit, a light, did not halt.

So let us celebrate these women of might,
Their stories, a testament to their fight,
Their courage, a beacon, did not die,
Their love, a river, did not dry.

CHILDREN

Sislin Fay Allen
by Eshan Ambrose

I am Sislin Fay Allen,
Here to fight crime.
Have you heard of me?
People treated me like grime.

I am Black,
And surprise, surprise, a Police Officer too.
Do you know, I quickly caught the knack,
At chasing after YOU.

I am Sislin Fay Allen,
Part of Windrush, did you know?
With my burglar-busting talent
I sailed high and took out dirty so-and-sos.

Don't get me wrong,
I enjoy being an inspiration to the next generation.
But sometimes, showing off,
Never felt true.

I am Sislin Fay Allen,
Marching to the beat,

Making life better,
For EVERYONE I meet.

Bringing down rowdy robbers and catching criminals,
These are just some of my special skills.
I'm not the kind to wear fancy frills,
And chances of escaping me are virtually nil.

I am Sislin Fay Allen,
First woman Black Officer.
I took another big step for equal rights,
So don't forget me (I KNOW WHERE YOU LIVE)!

YOUNGER TEENS

Be Black and Proud
by Lannaya Wilks

Black is Beautiful,
Black is Pain.

If Black is so beautiful, then why are you ashamed?

Black is Love,
Black is Elegant,
Black is Pride.

Please do not deny
our efforts to try.

Appreciate my melanin, my unique appearance.
The full thickness of my hair,
the full thickness of my lips.
I am unapologetically me, without your interference.

We may do things differently to you;
jerk chicken, rice and peas,
but at the end of the day, it's red; we all bleed.

YOUNGER TEENS

Mary Seacole: While the Bombshells Fall
by Isabella Hope-Smith

While the bombshells fall,
While the soldiers call,
When blood is seeping through the clothes,
When eyes are to forever close.

The sound of her footsteps fills the air,
Her mothering murmurs to show her care,
Mary Seacole takes a seat,
And mends the wounds until complete.

Although Mary re-opened eyes,
And saved each precious life,
People judged her for her skin colour,
Their bullets hit harsher than any other.

But she was strong, and from within,
She knew her colour was no sin,
So she continued saving lives,
The superhero of her time.

And so, while the bombshells fell,
There was never a 'farewell',
Blood stopped gushing at Mary's touch,
Until her golden time was up.

YOUNGER TEENS

Celebrate Black History
by Tehrim Fatima

In the heart of October's grace,
We celebrate a vibrant space,
Black history shines a brilliant light,
Guiding us through the darkest night.

From Harriet's courage, strong and free,
To Langston's words that set minds free,
Dr King's dream, a beacon so bright,
Injustice challenged with all their might.

Maya's poems, like birds in flight,
And Malcolm X, with words of might,
They paved the way with strength and art,
African roots are deep in every heart.

Through struggle, triumph, and unity,
Black history is a proud tapestry,
For every voice that fought and sang,
In this rich heritage, we all belong.

YOUNGER TEENS

SHE
by Narcisca Zaharia

One day, a black lady entered the bus.
SHE got ordered to the back of the bus.
But SHE was proud of her colour.
Proud of her race.
Determined not to suffer this disgrace,
SHE dug deep.
In the front, SHE remained.
SHE is Rosa Parks.

YOUNGER TEENS

Mary Seacole
by Jack Holland

Mother to the injured in the Crimean War.
Adored by those she nursed who were sore.
Rebuked by Florence Nightingale due to the colour of her skin.
Yearned to help, so she started her own inn.
Saved so many lives at the British hotel.
Every soldier, no matter who fell.
Achieved so much through her own good will.
Creole healing arts, rather than a pill.
Overcoming prejudice to achieve her goals.
Lauded now for saving so many souls.
Eternally remembered for her great love to all.

YOUNGER TEENS

The Magazine
by Lili Guthrie

The magazine gave her hope until the war came to a stop.
It twirled, and it danced into the hands of an orphan who wanted a chance.
Her name was Michela, and that was her name,
it would be spoken all over and said throughout fame.
But this little girl was different in a way,
her skin was the night but with patches of light
and maps on her skin that made people afraid.
But with Mina by her side, nothing would get in their way,
along with a new mother, she would be proud to say,
'I am a ballet dancer, a good one indeed
and I will inspire children of all colours and creeds.'

YOUNGER TEENS

Saluting Sisters:
A Tribute to Black Women in History
by Nosheen Akhtar

We salute the sisters who have paved the way
For us to shine and thrive in every domain
We honour their courage, their wisdom, their grace
And we celebrate their legacy that remains.

We salute the sisters who have fought for our rights
Like Rosa Parks, who refused to give up her seat
Like Harriet Tubman, who led slaves to the light
Like Sojourner Truth, who spoke truth to the elite.

We salute the sisters who have inspired us with their art
Like Maya Angelou, who wrote with beauty and power
Like Oprah Winfrey, who touched millions with her heart
Like Beyoncé, who dazzled us with her glamour.

We salute the sisters who have advanced our knowledge
Like Mae Jemison, who soared into space

Like Katherine Johnson, who did the maths for NASA
Like Marie Daly, who broke barriers in science.

We salute the sisters who have made a difference in the world
Like Mary Seacole, who nursed the wounded in the war
Like Diane Abbott, who made history in Parliament
Like Malorie Blackman, who wrote stories to explore.

And there are many more who deserve recognition
For their contributions in various fields
They are the Saluting Sisters of Black History Month
And their legacy never yields.

They are the black women who empower
The future generations
They are the ones who light the fire
The ones who spark the inspiration.

YOUNGER TEENS

Women Empowerment
by Summer Casson

Maya Angelou found her voice.
Rosa Parks made her choice.
Serena and Venus always aim high.
Simone Biles can touch the sky.
Michelle Obama will stand her case.
Alek Wek is more than a pretty face
From buses to tennis and flipping
From writing to speaking and dancing
I need to say one more thing
Thank you, women, for everything!

YOUNGER TEENS

Imagine...
by Eliza Krause

Imagine leading hundreds of slaves,
To freedom and a life of their own,
But being completely overlooked,
Rather than be recognised and shown.

Imagine being a soldier,
Fighting in a deadly and dangerous war,
But being seen as only your gender,
Rather than the things you helped to restore.

Imagine still today,
How many courageous people sacrifice it all,
But being seen as only a colour,
Rather than their heart and soul.

Imagine being Harriet Tubman,
A black woman and much more,
Her perseverance unmatchable,
And her story is something you shouldn't ignore.

YOUNGER TEENS

She Is
by Grace-Petra Quainoo-Abban

Ghana, what does she mean to me?
What closes the gaps in my family?
Ghana makes the roots
that grow, spread and turn
into my family tree.
From the colourful kente cloth
To the festive highlife songs,
My Ghanaian pride grows strong.

She is my Ghana
Deeply rooted in home, love, prayer and joy
She is my Ghana
My sweet melody of gospel songs ringing in the temple
of
My father's home
She is my Ghana
She is God's. She is His own.

How does she
Accept that this is a part of who she is
To not hide this truth

To not confine or change it?
This is my Ghana.

How does she
Become more than the stereotypes
Thrown carelessly at her
And love this hidden part of her?

This is my Ghana
dancing the night away
And swaying
to the rhythm of my ancestor's drum
beating in my DNA
catching up with the billions of relatives
I have to pretend I've seen it before today
This is my Ghana,
But this is my family.

This is my Ghana
She is the star, always shining unappreciated.
She is the rain growing my seed.

She is my African queen,
Her hidden crown blessed by her heritage
Placed in the roots of my scalp
growing together
in marriage.

Her eyes watching over me
running through my veins
are the earth's natural beauty
a knife sugar-coated in honey.

She is my Ghana
rich and deep, like dark chocolate
hidden well but not the smallest
her eyes hold the gold buried in the ground
blessed and holy, not just brown.

She is my Ghana
her scent of royalty, cocoa butter and love
are a silent welcome embracing me in childhood.

Her hands are my backbone
Held together in prayer
Her mouth writing my story for me
Whenever I feel broken.

She is My Ghana
Her smile
has a gap that shows
the history of
My Ghanaian ancestors
Love grown.

My taste buds cry
Tears of delight as
My soul opens,
Ready to get a taste,
of my Ghanaian side .

The servery bursting with foods from Ghana.
All families bring tastes
of childhood memories
made from mamas.

My mother is my Ghana
the roots
that grow, spread and turn
into my family tree.
She showed me
what Ghana means to me
the food, the culture, the history,
the family, the values of the community.
She helped my love for Ghana grow and grow
Like a weed that had found its proper place.

So, my mother is the calm before the storm
The sweet melody of gospel songs
The sun at the beginning and end of my day
Teaching my newborn lips to pray.

Her words of comfort and patience leading me
Holding me tight
So I don't go astray.

Her eyes
Are the angels righteously judging
Free and bold like a lion
Blessed and holy from my father
Soft and strict like a mother.

As she holds me,
the memories spark like the candles
She lit up on her cakes
Lighting up the night.

Her eyebrows are cupid bows
raised and arched, ready to shoot arrows
of love
piercing the heart
showing her truth
she is my Ghana.

YOUNGER TEENS

Sitting Down to Stand Up – Rosa Parks
by Darci Lee-Smith

In the face of injustice, Rosa Parks took a stand,
A courageous woman, with principles so grand.
She sat down to stand up for what was right,
A beacon of courage, shining through the night.

On that bus in Montgomery, she made her mark,
With a simple act, she ignited a spark.
Her refusal to yield her seat that day,
Became a symbol of the price she'd pay.

Arrested, but unbroken, she paved the way,
For a movement that would change night into day.
Her quiet strength and unwavering grace,
Inspires me to stand up in the face of any race.

Rosa Parks, an inspiration, a hero so true,
Her actions remind us of what we can do.
To challenge oppression, with courage we must,
And fight for justice, in her footsteps, we trust.

She taught us that change can start with one,
That justice and equality can be won.
Rosa, your legacy will forever be,
An inspiration to all, for eternity.

YOUNGER TEENS

We are Black Women
by Isabelle Ahanon

I am black and black is me,
I am proud of who I am, you see:
Because of strong women like Harriet Tubman,
I can celebrate my identity.

I am black and black is me,
I am proud of who I am, you see:
Because Rosa Parks paved the way,
Black women have the final say.

I am black and black is me,
I am proud of who I am, you see:
Never again will we fear to speak up,
For that we can thank Michelle Obama for doing as such.

I am black and black is me,
I am proud of who I am, you see:
Our hair is different, but who said you can touch it?
Braids and afros will stay as they are, it's the world that we live in that need to change, by far.

I am black and black is me,
I am proud of who I am, you see:
Never again shall we back out and run,
Because of the achievements and prizes black women have won.

I am black and black is me,
I am proud of who I am, you see:
For years and years black women have been denied,
That was before a black woman decided it's our time to shine!

YOUNGER TEENS

From a Black Girl to a Black Woman
by Yvette Wamala

From a black girl to a black woman,
I can't believe how far we've come,
From Rosa Parks to Amanda Gorman,
From Harriet Tubman to Michelle Obama,
It's crazy how time has turned the tables.

From a black girl to a black woman
I wish I was there.
Not for the racism,
Not for the discrimination,
But for the experience.

From a black girl to a black woman
I take dignity in my ancestor,
Whether small or big
Whether alive or dead.

Although it still happens
I'm proud of how we handled it,

Whether physical or verbal
We still made a change.
From a black girl to a black woman
I'm glad we taking steps into the right direction.

OLDER TEENS

Shine
by Elizabeth Okunola

We now live in a world where colours dance,
Where black women need to shine and be given a chance.
Their knowledge and abilities come so rare,
Where others are unable to compare.
Throughout history, they've tried, and they've fought
The history which needs to be retaught.
Their wisdom, courage and pride
Something they've often been told to hide.
In every field, they've been able to make their mark
But be careful not to cause a bark.
Their influence has been widely spread
Although some can't get it in their head.

Let's celebrate our dreams and goals,
As there is treasure within our souls.
Our worth and power to be cherished
And that way, our equality will never be perished.

OLDER TEENS

Grace
by Ronav Bhanot

In history's pages, a name we find,
A pioneering black woman, one of a kind.
With strength and grace, she blazed her trail,
Her legacy's power is like a mighty sail.

Through trials and struggles, she rose above,
An unwavering spirit filled with love.
She shattered barriers, broke through the night,
Guiding others toward a future so bright.

Her courage inspired, her wisdom profound,
In a world that once tried to keep her bound.
She fought for justice with passion; she'd speak,
A voice for the voiceless, both strong and meek.

In the face of adversity, she stood tall,
Breaking down walls, breaking every thrall.
Her journey's a beacon, a guiding star,
A pioneering black woman, near and far.

With vision and purpose, she led the way,
A hero, a trailblazer, in the light of day.
Her name will endure, a story to tell,
A pioneering black woman who rose and excelled.

OLDER TEENS

This Black Soul
by Natasha Gachuma

In this strange diaspora, I stand,
A black soul in a foreign land.
A tapestry of my family's history that I weave,
A tale of unfathomable strength, that is to be believe.

From my motherland's embrace I'm torn,
Yet, in my heart, her rhythm is born.
In the echoes of ancestral cries,
I tried to find the strength, but I –

Being black but far from home,
The struggle's real, and I know I'm not alone.
Sometimes it's hard, but I know I,
Carry Africa's pride in my ev'ry stride.

But here, the air is different, new,
A foreign world, a different hue.
They ask me where I'm really from,
As if my roots are something of a conundrum.

I tell them stories of my kin,
Of cultures rich, a world within,
I am a blend of old and new,
A fusion of the past and present, too.

Being black abroad, it's not a game,
For everywhere I go, I bear a name.
A legacy of strength and resilience,
With a hint of grace and brilliance.

Passed down through every generation's face,
A feeling of envy which is hard to place.

Then I see my people, stood strong and proud,
Creating communities and speaking aloud.
We stretch out our hands for those who can't reach,
Uniting hearts and breaking boundaries.

Yet there are moments when I ache,
For the land from which I partake.
The taste of nyama choma and plantain fried,
Reminds me of where my heart resides.

But being black and far from home,
It's a journey of growth, as I've known.
For I am a beacon of aspiration and a source of light,
Guiding others through their darkest night.

Juxtaposing the person who had been prior;
The young girl who'd dim her fire to suit other people's desire.

I wear my melanin with pride,
A testament to the strength inside.
Being black, no matter where I am,
Is a beautiful thread in this global strand.

So;
In this foreign land, I thrive,
A black soul with dreams that are alive.
I carry my roots, my heritage so grand,
For I am black, and I finally understand.

OLDER TEENS

Saluting our Sisters
by Lorna Kerr

The end of an era is closing; I turn the key in the lock,
And walk away from the law firm, the law that Mum Bett once studied.
Suing for freedom, she won, victorious! Despite the swarm of furious WASPs.
Turning around, I face that building and I salute, I salute Mum Bett.

Walking away from the past, the bus looms out of the shadows.
Sat in the crowd of smoke and gum, I remember the bravery of Rosa Parks.
Claiming her spot in history – she would not budge, not to the white men's anger.
In the stuffy bus, I raise my hand, and I salute.

Shivering, I hurry to the tube and am alone on an empty platform.
I stare into the gaping maw of darkness and venerate Harriet Tubman.

Facing the dark and walking miles, she freed her family from the clutches of the light-
Skinned men that held her. I revere her, and I salute the shadows.

Nearing the end of my venture, I huddle in my seat.
Eerily alone, I pull out a book, and I remember the ferocity of Audre Lorde.
Powerful and dangerous, her words reversed the hate of nations, her voice a beacon.
Until cancer struck her down, my tears wet the page, and I salute her.

I walk the rest of the way, staring at the stars.
Almost into the warmth, I stop on the brink and turn to the night.
I remember all the brave women, no, soldiers, who wrote a new course of history.
I turn to the world, and I salute our sisters.

OLDER TEENS

Michelle Obama
by Dora Glass

Michelle Obama, a woman of grace,
Inspiring us all with her strong embrace.
She is an advocate for health and education,
A role model for a great nation.

Michelle Obama, a beacon of light,
Empowering women with all her might.
Her passion for justice, equality, and more,
Leaves us all inspired to reach for the stars and soar.

OLDER TEENS

Whispers of Anastacia
by Pakeeza Noor

In the pages of history, a name concealed,
Escrava Anastacia, her story unrevealed,
A forgotten Black woman, a silent cry,
In the shadow of oppression, she dared to fly.

Born into bondage, her spirit unbound,
In a world of chains, a voice profound,
Escrava Anastacia, her name we now recall,
A symbol of resilience despite it all.

In the heart of Brazil, where her tale did unfold,
She carried her burdens, her stories untold,
With dignity and grace, she faced the pain,
In the depths of injustice, she did remain.

Her face marked by beauty, adorned with a band,
The iron crown of suffering, a cruel brand,
Escrava Anastacia, a symbol of strength,
In her silent defiance, her spirit found its length.

Her life is a testament to the power within,
In the face of adversity, she refused to give in,

A forgotten Black woman, we remember her today,
For her enduring spirit, in our hearts, will stay.

Though time may have hidden her from view,
Escrava Anastacia, we honour you,
In the annals of history, your name we'll inscribe,
A symbol of courage in which we confide.

OLDER TEENS

My Identity
by Princess Martins

My Identity
won't let me be,
but here I lie so called freely,
with "peace".
The "peace" of having to watch my back
or yet so as not to be too black.
The "peace" of learning Caucasian people's history
whilst I'm still wondering about mine.
Why there is no equality will always be a mystery
cause black is great
and black is beauty
and yet we are still shamed,
made to feel like we have to carry the weight of being black,
they try to make being black a pain.
My skin will not be the reason I fail but why I achieve my destiny,
lighter skin may get you your way
but melanin is where the sun lays
and that's why we shine all day,
yet you call us out when our hair is not layered
cause it looks too wild and untamed

but the texture and coils remain,
just like how we still stay here fighting for equality within our race,
the workplace and society nowadays.
But the real question is, why am I proud to be a young black female?
My culture is what lies behind me
deep inside me, but it does not define me
but it takes up a side of me.
My race is something that I'll never change,
even when I have to work 10x harder, I'll do it with grace
cause we all know they need someone like us up on that stage
but your race is not you.
You are your race,
use it as your superpower.
No matter what colour, in the end, we all come together,
even through the struggles we may face.
Always remember that this is our adventure
that lies within the heart,
and this black tale will forever enlighten your day.
cause this is real life and I'm here to stay,
and I'm not playing no games.
No matter what you say I am worthy and this is my life's journey,
and I decide when my story ends.

OLDER TEENS

Her Hidden History
by Felicity Whele-Plummer

To the women who achieved brilliance,
who went the extra mile and showed great resilience.
Who fought for the rights of others
Yet their stories remain a mystery
A Hidden part of history.
The truth of the other side,
The truth of the other half of me.

She refused to give up her seat and ordered to move,
firmly planting her feet.
In an act of defiance, she broke the law, and civil rights
protesters were in uproar.

She, whose son was killed by the park,
Challenged the justice system and made her mark
She founded the Stephen Lawrence Society,
campaigning tirelessly

Appointed an OBE for her service to the community,
She, who was the first trans-gay liberator,
raising awareness, there were many like her

The P in her name stands for "pay it no mind", as she did the majority of her life
Creating STAR, a safe haven for black trans youth
a place for minorities seeking their inner truth.

She, who was the first gymnast to win four gold medals in history,
showcasing her immense prowess and ability
The first African American woman to win an all-around title
Her contributions to gymnastics were ground-breaking and vital.

She came to Britain to gain her education
A nursing degree was her inspired vocation
Specialising in over nine medical fields,
she taught and trained those how to care for and heal.
She achieved her medical degree,
The first black woman in my history

She, who gained a degree in Psychology
Studying and graduating at the West Indies University
Because of her race, there was a stereotype
So, she used her work to support others in their fight
Always needing to overachieve, she gained an incredible four degrees.

Who are they? Claudette, Doreen, Marsha and Simone
The first few hidden in view
The last two unknown to all of you.

A true matriarch Merl, my grandma from Jamaica
My Auntie Charmaine, a great teacher and educator.

These women no longer a mystery,
A hidden part of History
These women they live on through me
Their rightfully recognised History.

OLDER TEENS

Black History Month
by Pranav Yadav

In history's tapestry, a tale unfolds,
Of strength and grace in stories left untold.
A black woman, resilient and bold,
Her legacy, a treasure, is worth more than gold.

In ancient Africa, where her roots began,
She bore the weight of history's cruel plan,
Through trials and tribulations, she'd stand,
A symbol of endurance across the land.

From Harriet Tubman's daring flight,
Guiding slaves to freedom through the darkest night,
To Sojourner Truth, with words so right,
She fought for justice, with unwavering might.

Rosa Parks, on that fateful bus seat,
Challenged the system, her spirit replete,
With courage, she'd not accept defeat,
A spark in the struggle, her act so sweet.

Maya Angelou's words, like birds in flight,
Lifted souls with their wisdom and insight,

Her poetry is a beacon in the night,
A black woman's voice, shining so bright.

In sciences, too, her brilliance shines,
Like Katherine Johnson's maths, in space designs,
A hidden figure among the stars aligns,
A black woman's genius, our world defines.

In every field, her contributions grow,
From politics to art, she's helped us to know,
That strength and beauty in her spirit flow,
A black woman in history, her legacy aglow.

So let us celebrate, honour and revere,
The black women whose stories are crystal clear,
Their history, a testament to persevere,
A legacy of courage, love and no fear.

OLDER TEENS

Inspirational Black Women
by Sabooh Ahmed

In honour of Black History Month's embrace,
Let's celebrate the strength and grace,
Of inspirational black women, history's gems,
Whose unique stories, we'll now proclaim.

Rosa Parks, a symbol of courage and might,
Her brave stand for justice, a shining light,
A unique act of resistance, a turning tide,
She took a seat at the front, stood with pride.

Harriet Tubman, a beacon in the night,
Guiding slaves to freedom, her spirit so bright,
Her unique path in the Underground Rail
Helped countless souls break their jail.

Maya Angelou, she wrote of courage and hope,
Soothing others, as they turned to her to cope,
With a graceful voice, she'd rise and sing,
Of the caged bird's freedom, with its vibrant wing.

Serena Williams, a story of resilience,
Overcoming challenges with relentless brilliance,

On the court, her power and skill on display,
Winning the hearts of all, in every way.

Inspirational Black women, their stories combined,
In this special month, their legacy's entwined,
They stood, and stand, bold and true,
Their stories, our history, a tribute to you.

ADULTS

Afraid to be Alone, but Wanting to be Free
by Rebecca McLeod

I will speak my truth and shout it out loud.
No matter the content, I hold my head up proud.
Shame has incapacitated me for far too long.
Never did I believe in my own redemption song.

Fear is an emotion that kept me small.
I responded defensively or curled up in a ball.
It kept me in relationships that were harmful to me.
Afraid to be alone, yet wanting to be free.

Partners preyed upon my fear and vulnerability.
Taking power and control, they walked all over me.
Physical, emotional and financial abuse left me broken.
A threatening presence loomed over me with words unspoken.

The gaslighting caused me to question my memory recall.
Did it happen that way, or is this insanity after all?
You're over emotional; that's what I was told.
When this 'crazy' woman tried to break the hold.
Afraid to be alone, yet wanting to be free.

I said 'NO' to fear and took steps towards becoming me.
No longer a caged bird, I have taken time to heal.
I rediscovered my identity and my authentic self I reveal.

I am limitless; fear and shame can no longer hold me down.
As a black queen, I stand in my power and adjust my crown.

Black History Month magazine is available from
www.blackhistorymonth.org.uk

Follow us on social media:
(X) @BHMUK
(In) @BHM_UK

www.ingramcontent.com/pod-product-compliance
Lightning Source LLC
Chambersburg PA
CBHW050239120526
44590CB00016B/2149